Pope Francis

IN IRELAND

COMMEMORATIVE SOUVENIR

First published in 2018 by
COLUMBA BOOKS
23 Merrion Square
Dublin 2, Ireland
www.columbabooks.com

ISBN: 978 1 78218 350 1

Set in Adobe Garamond Pro and Lato
Cover and book design by Alba Esteban | Columba Books

Front cover image by Stephen McCarthy/Sportsfile via Getty Images
and back cover image by Maxwells/WMOF2018
Printed by Jellyfish Solutions

POPE FRANCIS
IN IRELAND

COMMEMORATIVE SOUVENIR

columba
BOOKS

CONTENTS

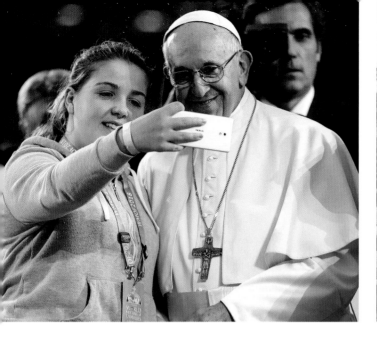

CLOCKWISE FROM ABOVE:

Pope Francis takes a 'selfie' with Alison Nevin, aged 12, during the Festival of Families.

Marie Walsh, Sarah O'Leary, Imelda O'Leary, Barry O'Leary, Margaret O'Leary, David O'Leary, Dennis O'Leary and Ronan O'Leary awaiting the Pope's arrival at the Phoenix Park.

A little girl waves a papal flag as the Pope arrives in the Phoenix Park for the closing Mass.

Pope Francis blesses Bella Hartigan, aged 11 months, with her mother Candice, at the Capuchin Day Centre on Bowe Street in Dublin.

Members of the congregation at the closing Mass in the Phoneix Park greet the Pope.

Photos by Maxwells/WMOF2018

"As families, you are the hope of the Church and of the world! God, Father, Son and Holy Spirit, created mankind in his image and likeness to share in his love, to be a family of families, and to enjoy the peace that he alone can give. By your witness to the Gospel, you can help God's dream to come true. You can help to draw all God's children closer together, so that they can grow in unity and learn what it is for the entire world to live in peace as one great family."

POPE FRANCIS
Festival of Families, Dublin, 25th August 2018

FOREWORD

In January 2014, a piece of graffiti art appeared on a wall close to the Vatican. The mural cartoon was the work of Maupal, a popular Italian artist, and depicted Pope Francis flying into the air clutching a small black case on which was written the word, "values".

The drawing summed up the favourable opinion people had of the Pope who had been elected ten months earlier. The previous month Pope Francis had been voted *Time* magazine's Man of the Year and featured on the cover.

I have a vivid memory of the evening Pope Francis was elected when I stood with thousands of others in St Peter's Square. The unexpected abdication of Pope Benedict XVI in February had caused a degree of uncertainty and anxiety throughout the Church. The octogenarian Pontiff had decided that his waning energy left him unable to lead the Church for much longer. He therefore decided to abdicate before his strength deteriorated further and to allow for a new Pope to take the helm.

The 115 cardinals who gathered in conclave for the second pontifical election of the third millennium were anxious for a smooth and rapid transition. After just one day's deliberation, they chose the 76-year-old Jesuit Archbishop of Buenos Aires who had already been one of the favoured candidates at the conclave which had elected Benedict XVI in 2005.

OPPOSITE: Pope Francis waves to the crowds at Knock Shrine. *Photo: Maxwells/WMOF2018.*

The bells across Rome pealed as white smoke billowed from a chimney in the roof of the Sistine Chapel where the cardinal electors had reached their decision. An hour after Cardinal Jean Louis Tauran announced the news to the crowds that a new Pope had been chosen, Pope Francis appeared on the balcony. The cheers and applause for this relatively unknown cardinal were extraordinary. A Latin American, with Italian heritage, he won the hearts of people as he greeted them with an informal "*buonsera*".

From the beginning of the pontificate, Francis let his priorities be known. A few weeks after his election, he celebrated the Mass of the Lord's Supper on Holy Thursday in a juvenile detention centre. The Mass had traditionally been celebrated in the sumptuous surroundings of Rome's cathedral of St John Lateran. During the Mass the Pope washed the feet of young girls and boys, including two Muslims. The ritual recalls the gesture of Jesus who washed the feet of his apostles at the Last Supper, offering them an example of service to follow.

Pope Francis seems little daunted by the challenges he faces as he leads the world's 1.3 billion Catholics. He does not hold up the teachings of Jesus as a remote set of ideals towards which people must strive. He believes the Church should meet people where they are at, often in the difficult and complex moments of everyday life. When referring to the Church, he likes to use the expression "a field hospital". Christians are called to be holy, but Francis understands well that the call is challenging and often we fall far from the mark.

There are two themes which are clearly close to Francis' heart, migration and human trafficking. Just three months after his election the Pope made his first trip outside the Vatican, choosing to visit the small island of Lampedusa in the Mediterranean Sea. There is little to see on the island but in recent years it has been overwhelmed by migrants from Africa fleeing war, drought, famine and poverty in the hopes of building a better life in Europe. The Arab Spring in North Africa of 2011-12, whereby the local populace had risen against governments, had led to political instability and forced migration.

During the day trip to Lampedusa, the Pope met with both refugees and islanders and celebrated Mass on a boat which had been used by pirates to transport the human cargo. Several such vessels regularly capsized with the loss of hundreds of lives. Over the coming months Pope Francis appealed to governments not "to turn the Mediterranean into a cemetery".

Pope Francis asked the Pontifical Academy for the Sciences to work with global governments and institutions to help tackle human trafficking and global warming. For Francis, the two are linked and lead to avoidable poverty. I attended a session organised by the Galileo Foundation which brought together mayors and governors from across the globe to examine the complex issues. Pope Francis attended the closing session at the Casina Pia IV in the Vatican and spoke about the need for close cooperation to try and improve the situation. He has a particular style when speaking. He begins in a very low voice which forces the listener to concentrate, before gradually rising to a normal level. He rarely uses speeches prepared for him, preferring to speak off the cuff. As I listened to him, I thought of his own background, the son of Italian migrants. He knew well what sacrifices are required in the search for a better and more secure life.

At the end of the conference, the Pope was due to meet the politicians who had come from seventy cities on five continents. He duly shook hands with some of the dignitaries. However, his face lit up when two young girls were presented to him. They came from Mexico. One had been sold by her impoverished parents into prostitution while the other had worked in a sweatshop, ironing clothes in a factory for up to 12 hours a day. Both had been liberated by the Mexican police. The Pope spent quite a while with them and there were many tears. Meanwhile the politicians had to wait patiently to have a group photograph. The Pope insisted that the girls stand beside him for the official photograph.

Pope Francis has no delusions of grandeur. A Jesuit for most of his life, he is used to austerity and simplicity. When asked in an interview how to best describe himself, he paused for a few moments before answering, "I am a sinner". It was not an empty claim. He has often explained that he does not trust his first reactions, which are usually wrong. He has to think a lot about the correct thing to do. He has made grave mistakes, most notably in dealing with victims in Chile who were abused by a priest and for whom bishops covered up. During a visit to that country he stated that he had no proof that their allegations were true. When he discovered the truth, he invited them to Rome so that he could apologise privately to each individual.

The visit to Ireland was overshadowed by the scandal of clerical sexual abuse and the way in which for decades the abuse had been covered up. Francis met with eight abuse survivors at the Apostolic Nunciature in Dublin. During the hour and a half meeting the Pope listened intently and pledged to eradicate such abuse from the Church. At the suggestion of one of the group, he publicly begged forgiveness the next day at the closing Mass in the Phoenix Park for the way in which Church figures abused the minds, bodies and consciences of vulnerable people, in particular unmarried mothers and the children from whom they were separated almost at birth.

During Pope Francis' visit to Ireland for the World Meeting of Families, you may have followed the events on television, radio or newspapers. You probably have your own favourite image. This book may capture the sentiment of that moment and bring back to mind happy memories of those days at the end of August when our nation rejoiced in offering hospitality to the thousands who came to visit us.

c. Michael Collins 2018

INTRODUCTION

The Irish Church has just experienced an incredible boost in faith thanks to a historic papal visit and the events of the World Meeting of Families 2018 in Dublin.

Held every three years, this major international event brings together families from across the world to celebrate, pray and discuss the vital importance of marriage and the family as the foundation for our society and our Church.

For 2018, Pope Francis chose the Archdiocese of Dublin to host the event, guided by the theme 'The Gospel of the Family: Joy for the World'.

Thousands of families and individuals from all over Ireland and the world attended the event and this book sets out to capture some of their experiences and to commemorate these extraordinary, joyful few days.

It also captures our first papal visit in almost 40 years, with Pope Francis attending a packed itinerary ranging from civic formalities to meetings with abuse survivors and the homeless, to large events such as the Festival of Families in Croke Park and the closing Mass in the Phoenix Park.

I would like to thank the diocesan representatives, the editorial team at *The Irish Catholic*, the team at Columba Books and all the photographers nationwide who made this beautiful book possible.

Mags Gargan
Managing Editor, Columba Books
August 2018

OPPOSITE: A child waves a Vatican flag as Pope Francis makes his way through the crowd at Croke Park. *Photo: Maxwells/WMOF2018*

It's estimated

750,000

people in total attended all the WMOF events, from the opening ceremonies in each diocese to the Pope's final Mass in the Phoenix Park.

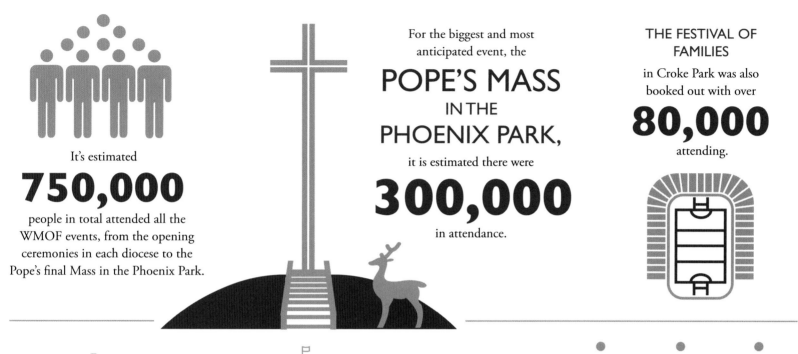

For the biggest and most anticipated event, the

POPE'S MASS
IN THE
PHOENIX PARK,

it is estimated there were

300,000

in attendance.

THE FESTIVAL OF
FAMILIES

in Croke Park was also booked out with over

80,000

attending.

All

45,000

TICKETS FOR KNOCK
were booked out in just
FOUR HOURS
by excited pilgrims.

About

37,000

people descended
on the RDS
from Wednesday-Friday for the
Pastoral Congress.
A huge amount of these

- 15,000 -

came from 116 COUNTRIES.

292
ANNOUNCED SPEAKERS

91
lay women

65
lay men

44
clergy/religious

In total **6,000 young people** under 18 attended the Pastoral Congress, with all areas of the event being family friendly. A further **2,000 performers** kept all entertained.

Finally it is thanks to the

7,000 volunteers

from all over Ireland, who agreed to give their time to make the event a success, that the WMOF has been made possible.

POPE FRANCIS IN PROFILE

From the moment he stepped onto the balcony of St Peter's Basilica after his election to the papacy on March 13, 2013, Pope Francis has captured the world's attention with his simple message of God's boundless love and mercy. His is a Church for the poor, a maternal Church keen to take care of all its followers. He combines a fidelity to the Church's teaching on key issues like marriage and hospitality with a lively love for the poor and the vulnerable. He is a pope who, in a world obsessed with power and prestige, represents the voiceless.

Pope Francis was born Jorge Mario Bergoglio in Buenos Aires, Argentina on December 17, 1936. He is one of five children born to Regina María Sivori and Mario José Bergoglio, who was an Italian immigrant from Turin in northern Italy. His father left Italy in his early 20s, moving with his parents to Argentina to pursue work in paving. His father and grandparents' journey from Italy to Argentina deeply impressed upon Jorge the importance of advocating for migrants, which he has done time and time again while in the papal office, even dedicating his 2018 New Year appeal to the issue; he implored people to "embrace" migrants and refugees to ensure a "peaceful future" for everyone.

Rosa Bergoglio, Pope Francis' grandmother, was also hugely influential on the future Pope's life. Rosa was a profoundly religious woman. While living in Italy, she gave speeches and organised events to promote the social teachings of popes, and afterward, while living in Argentina, she told her grandson Jorge all about her involvement in Catholic Action, a network of active lay Catholics in Italy. His grandmother's keen faith and obvious devotion to the Church influenced Pope Francis, who from a young age was strong in his religious faith. The family's parish priest, Fr Enrico Pozzoli, was also a regular at the Bergoglio family dinner table, which no doubt further influenced Pope Francis' burgeoning interest in the Christian faith.

The Pope's family was not wealthy, but neither did they want for life's necessities. They were happy with their lot in life, and the influence of their humility is visible in the way Pope Francis lives his life; he prefers to live modestly and free of material excesses. As cardinal, he cooked his own meals in his small Buenos Aires apartment and always took the subway to get around the city. After assuming the papacy in 2013, he refused to live in the lavish papal apartments available to him, preferring a smaller, more humble abode. The day after being elected pope, he journeyed back to the Church guesthouse where he had stayed, greeting the workers at the hotel's front desk and paying his own bill, despite the fact that as the new leader of the Catholic Church, he technically controlled the guesthouse! During his 2015 trip to the United States, he surprised followers by riding around in an understated black Fiat, rather than the larger cars often favoured by visiting dignitaries and religious figures, a decision that was most likely a nod to his desire to promote environmentalism and

OPPOSITE: Pope Francis smiling on the stage at Croke Park. *Photo: Maxwells/WMOF2018.*

avoid what he calls "a culture of waste". He embodies the humility he stresses so fervently in his sermons and speeches, showing followers that it is indeed possible to be humble and tender, even in one of the most powerful positions in the world.

In addition to maintaining a close relationship with his grandmother, Pope Francis also got along well with his siblings, including Maria Elena, who is still alive today. Maria describes her brother as a funny, supportive sibling and friend who speaks with his actions as well as his words. A bright, enthusiastic student, Pope Francis studied food chemistry in high school, gaining a chemical technician's diploma. After high school, he worked in a laboratory, and it is here that he developed an interest in politics, thanks in large part to his boss at the time, Esther Ballestrino. Esther lent him books on left-wing politics that inspired him to explore the political clubs of Buenos Aires at the time. However, despite this interest he felt increasingly called to the vocation, realising a desire to enter the priesthood in 1953 while at confession. In 1958, he declared his intention to become a Jesuit priest and entered the order's seminary of Villa Devoto on March 11 of that year. Pope Francis had a nearly fatal health crisis shortly after entering the seminary. A severe bout of pneumonia caused him to suffer from painfully inflamed lung membranes, a condition also known as pleurisy that required surgery on and the partial removal of his right lung and three cysts. The Pope is still affected by this health scare; he's prone to colds and chest conditions and gets out of breath easily.

As part of his formation, the Pope studied liberal arts in Santiago, Chile. In 1960, he gained a Master's degree in philosophy from the Colegio Maximo de San Jose in Buenos Aires. He then taught literature and psychology at the Colegio de la Immaculada Concepcion in the Santa Fe province from 1964 to 1965, transferring a year later to the Colegio del Salvador in Buenos Aires, where he taught the same subjects. He finished his own theological studies in 1967 and in 1969 he was ordained.

Fr Bergoglio completed the final stage of his Jesuit spiritual training at Alcala de Henares in Spain, taking the fourth and final vow as a Jesuit in 1973. That same year, he was named provincial superior of the Jesuits in Argentina, a role he served in until 1979. Returning to teaching in 1980 in San Miguel, that same year he became rector of the Philosophical and Theological Faculty of San Miguel, until 1986. Pope Francis also visited Dublin for eight weeks in 1980 to learn English at the Jesuit Milltown Institute in Ranelagh.

After completing his doctoral dissertation in Germany that same year, he served as a confessor and spiritual director in Córdoba. In May 1992, he was named titular Bishop of Auca and Auxiliary Bishop of Buenos Aires and was consecrated on June 27 of that year. On June 3, 1997, he was named coadjutor archbishop of the archdiocese and subsequently installed as the new Archbishop of Buenos Aires on February 28, 1998. He took as his episcopal motto 'Miserando atque Eligendo' (Lowly and yet Chosen). Archbishop Bergoglio was elevated to cardinal during the consistory of February 21, 2001, receiving his biretta and his Roman Church of Jesuit St Robert Bellarmino from Pope John Paul II. He participated in the 2005 conclave to elect John Paul's successor, and is said to have come second to Cardinal Joseph Ratzinger, who became Pope Benedict XVI. Later in the year, on November 9, Cardinal Bergoglio was elected as President of the Epsicopal Conference of Argentina.

When Cardinal Bergoglio was elected Pope in 2013, he chose the name Francis in honour of St Francis of Assisi and his reputation for helping the poor. His sister Maria Elena says that her brother has always been committed to advocating for the poor, noting his dream to free the Church of money and privileges so that it can more fully understand and empathise with its followers.

OPPOSITE: Pope Francis as a young man.

TOP RIGHT: Pope Francis served as a cardinal from 2001-2013 in Argentina.

BOTTOM RIGHT: The Pope has always been humble; here he is pictured riding public transit in Argentina back when he was Cardinal Bergoglio.

The Pope has in fact devoted himself to supporting the world's impoverished population, establishing projects for inhabitants of Buenos Aires's Villa 21-24 slum during his time as cardinal. Thanks to his efforts, the slum was able to offer carpentry classes and initiate fundraising marathons to inhabitants to help them cultivate marketable skills and raise money for community works.

On Holy Thursday, 2016, Pope Francis visited Rome's Centre for Asylum Seekers and washed the feet of both male and female refugees at the centre. In 2017 the Pope also established Rome's first free laundrette to offer the city's poor the opportunity to wash, launder their clothes, get haircuts and seek medical care. In 2018 he sponsored an event that allowed the Vatican to bring a group of low-income families, refugees, prisoners and the homeless to an evening at the circus.

Like the modern popes before him, Pope Francis has made it his mission to visit as many countries as possible. In the past five years, Pope Francis has visited over 30 countries, among them: Brazil, Israel, Jordan, Sri Lanka, the Philippines, Albania, Germany, the United States, South Korea, France, Cuba, Armenia, Poland and Mexico. He is also the first pope to ever visit Myanmar. He is an extremely well travelled pope, having been to five different continents during his time in the papal office. This year he became the first pope to visit Ireland since Pope John Paul II visited in 1979.

It makes sense that the Pope's visit would centre on the family, since family is incredibly important to Pope Francis. He frequently vocalises the importance of the family as the basic building block of society and has said that the family "is the greatest treasure of any country". The Pope has even founded a new Institute on Marriage and Family in John Paul II's name, and his publication of *Amoris Laetitia* reaffirms the importance of the family unit in the eyes of the Catholic Church. In *Amoris Laetitia*, he notes, "Indeed the good of the family is decisive for the future of the world and of the Church." He views family as an antidote to isolation and uncertainty, saying that he prefers a "wounded family that makes daily efforts to put love into play to a society that is sick from isolationism and is habitually afraid of love".

In a 2017 speech at the Roma Tre University, the Pope told listeners that the cultivation of family starts at the dinner table, noting the importance of families sharing meals together free from the distractions of phones and other diverting devices. In addition to sharing meals together, Pope Francis also advocated in his Family Day Mass speech at St Peter's Square in 2013 that families also simply spend time supporting each other and getting to know one another, through both prayer and daily life, so that they can share joy together and incorporate faith into their everyday activities.

Pope Francis is confident that families are essential for the health of society both now and in the future as well.

Pope Francis washing the feet of women and men at a youth detention centre near Rome in 2013. *Photo: Catholic News Service*

LAST IRISH PAPAL VISIT

The last time a Pope came to Ireland was nearly 40 years ago, when Pope John Paul II visited from September 29 – October 1 in 1979. This papal visit was one of the most remarkable events in the history of the Irish State. For one, some 2.7 million people, almost half of the population of the island of Ireland at the time, attended Masses and liturgies with the Holy Father. Irish Catholics had been used to seeing the Pope as a distant figure in Rome, prayed for during Mass or seen on a rare pilgrimage to Rome. Here was this Slavic Pontiff, a mere 59-year-old, striding down the steps of Aer Lingus' flagship St Patrick. The moment he set foot on Irish soil he kissed the ground to huge cheers from those who had gathered. Even before he touched down, a decision to fly the papal plane low across Dublin thrilled the 1.25 million pilgrims gathered in the Phoenix Park.

His first day in Ireland, Pope John Paul celebrated a Mass in that same park that drew over 1 million people. He also visited the office of the President and celebrated a Liturgy of the Word for 300,000 people in Killineer, outside Drogheda in Co. Louth. On his second of three days in Ireland, the Pope visited Clonmacnoise monastery in Co. Offaly, a visit that was attended by 20,000 people. He also presided at a Youth Mass in Galway that attracted 300,000 people, and an outdoor Mass at Knock Shrine in Co. Mayo that was attended by 450,000 people. On his final day, the Pope visited St Patrick's College in Maynooth - the national seminary – and then celebrated a final Mass at Greenpark Racecourse in Limerick offered for the people of Munster.

The Troubles in Northern Ireland cast a long shadow over the 1970s and in the aftermath of the murder of Earl Mountbatten and members of his family, along with the Warrenpoint killings only weeks earlier, the Pope was forced to avoid the North entirely during his visit. In his homily during the Mass at Drogheda, which is in the Archdiocese of Armagh, he called on the paramilitaries to lay down their arms:

"Now I wish to speak to all men and women engaged in violence. I appeal to you, in language of passionate pleading. On my knees I beg you to turn away from the paths of violence and to return to the ways of peace. You may claim to seek justice. I too believe in justice and seek justice. But violence only delays the day of justice. Violence destroys the work of justice. Further violence in Ireland will only drag down to ruin the land you claim to love and the values you claim to cherish."

It was always a regret of John Paul's that he was unable to see the North and right up to the time of his death in 2005, there were tentative plans to make a short visit there.

Pope John Paul II was the first non-Italian Pope in over 400 years, and the second longest-reigning Pope in history. He was passionate about human rights and helped bring about the end of communism in his native Poland. He also emphasised the importance of family to his fellow religious and followers, organising an Ordinary General Assembly of the Synod of Bishops in 1980 to discuss the Christian family. He also established the Pontifical Council for the Family, on May 9, 1981. His most important act supporting Christian families is, of course, the establishment of the tri-annual World Meeting of Families in 1994. Pope John Paul II attended three of these meetings himself, and now Pope Francis continues the tradition.

OPPOSITE: Pope John Paul II waves to the crowds in the Phoenix Park during the 1979 papal visit.

Some of the festivities during the
Opening Ceremony in Armagh
Photo: www.LiamMcArdle.com

WORLD MEETING
OF FAMILIES
PREPARATIONS

ICON OF THE HOLY FAMILY

E ach World Meeting of Families has its own iconic image to encourage reflection and prayer that is unique to that particular year's event. The World Meeting of Families 2018 specially commissioned Icon of the Holy Family was unveiled and anointed on the 21st August 2017 at the National Novena in Knock, Co. Mayo. Archbishop Diarmuid Martin, President of World Meeting of Families 2018, led the celebration to launch the year-long programme of festivities leading up to the WMOF2018, a programme that included the beginning of the icon's travels. The archbishop called the programme, "a call to renew the Church so that it can enter into a new future: a future in which our Church will attract more and more people to Jesus".

The icon is made of seasoned wood and was written by iconographer Mihai Cucu with assistance from the Redemptoristine Sisters of the Monastery of St Alphonsus in Dublin. The icon features an outer structure shaped like a house with double doors, on which are the angels Michael and Gabriel on the left and right. At the bottom of the doors are words that mean 'Joy of Love', which is the Pope's message to the faithful regarding the family. When the icon doors are opened, the Holy Family is visible celebrating Passover together, a meal that traditionally revolves around the family table. Surrounding the image of the Holy Family are images from the Gospels, featuring Jesus reviving the daughter of Jairus and helping a married couple at the Wedding Feast of Cana. These images show the importance that Jesus places on family life in the Bible.

In the year leading up to the WMOF2018, the icon was taken on a pilgrimage to visit the 26 dioceses on the island of Ireland. Many dioceses organised a special procession into their cathedral often led by a local celebrity or leading figure. The icon was then

The icon of World Meeting of Families is presented to the Pope in Rome during his general audience in St Peter's Square. The Pope is pictured here with Archbishop Diarmuid Martin, World Meeting of Families 2018 media manager Brenda Drumm, and one of the Irish families who travelled to greet the Pope with the icon. *Photo: Catholic News Service*

put on display in different parish churches in the diocese, until it departed for the next diocese after weekend Mass.

In the Diocese of Waterford and Lismore, Bishop Phonsie Cullinan held a special Holy Hour for Families in the Cathedral of the Most Holy Trinity during which he reflected on each of the images present in the icon and how they relate to family life today. A similar discussion was held in the Dublin parish of Ringsend during which Deacon Tom Groves explained the meaning of the icon's panels to the pupils of St Patrick's Boys and Girls National School. The parish of St Gabriel in Fingal South East, Dublin also involved local schoolchildren, who were invited to visit the icon.

Fr Eamon O'Gorman created a new tradition when he performed a special piece of music on the tin whistle to welcome the icon to the Diocese of Ossory, and it cannot be stressed how important the icon's visit to staff and prisoners in Midlands Prison in the Diocese of Kildare & Leighlin was, with Bishop Denis Nulty describing it as a "very graced and special moment".

A petition box also accompanied the icon on its travels, to gather family prayers and petitions throughout the year. These petitions were sent to contemplative orders all over Ireland, who remembered each petition in their prayers throughout the year. Prior to the World Meeting of Families itself, all the petitions were gathered up and brought to the Pope's closing Mass in the Phoenix Park.

Pope Francis was presented with the icon during his weekly general audience in St Peter's Square in Rome in March, 2018. It was also at this audience that the Pope confirmed his visit to Ireland. Two Irish families in a delegation led by WMOF2018 President, Archbishop Diarmuid Martin and Secretary General, Fr Timothy Bartlett presented the icon to the Pope.

OPPOSITE: Children from Listowel Presentation Primary School pictured with the Holy Family Icon in St Mary's Church, Listowel during the icon's visit to the Diocese of Kerry. *Photo: Denise Moran*

DIOCESAN PREPARATIONS

In preparation for the World Meeting of Families 2018, dioceses from all over Ireland organised gatherings to promote the event and the importance it places on the modern Christian family unit, through celebrations that engaged the local community. Many were inspired by the WMOF2018's 'Amoris: Let's Talk Family' programme, a collection of initiatives to help parishes integrate the theme of family into faith-based activities leading up to the event.

To help parishioners get into the festive spirit, family fun days cropped up in almost every diocese, both North to South, starting in 2017 and continuing throughout the spring and summer of 2018.

Bishop John Fleming from the Diocese of Killala hosted a Garden Fun Day in the front garden of his home to give his community a boost as they counted down the days to WMOF2018. The day included a bouncy castle, live music, treasure hunts and a massive barbecue.

The Archdiocese of Armagh also held a garden-focused event: a special Family Planting Day in the parish of Loughlilly that afforded families the opportunity to plant shrubs and bedding plants in a formerly neglected area of forested land. Armagh archdiocese also went off-piste and held a Family of Sport Celebration led by Archbishop Eamon Martin.

Thirty sport clubs attended the event, and participants were encouraged to wear their sporting jerseys to the celebration, which included a procession of clubs holding their flags and banners.

In the Diocese of Meath, the parish of Kinnegad held The Big Parish Picnic, an event for families in the area that included music, games, a gardening lecture and the annual Family Fun Cycle. Families from neighbouring parishes were invited and the parish advertised it as a 'technology-free' way to spend a few fun hours with the family.

The Diocese of Kildare & Leighlin held two similarly successful events – a Family Picnic Day at Punchestown Racecourse in 2017 and the Kandle Family Fun Day at Carlow College in 2018, which both drew huge crowds and featured arts and crafts, music, games, and even a bicycle obstacle course.

The inclement weather didn't stop the Family Picnic in Lough Key, in the Diocese of Elphin, from going forward. The event featured a brass band, multiple choirs and face painting.

The Family Fun Day held at Tipp Racecourse by the Cashel and Emly archdiocese also didn't stop, despite morning mist and forecasts for rain. The event featured a special 'Family Art Project' with contributions from families at every primary school in the diocese.

OPPOSITE: A family gathered with Bishop Brendan Leahy during the Limerick Diocesan Family Fun Day at Mary Immaculate College. *Photo: Keith Wiseman*

Parishioners from the Diocese of Killala visit Bishop Fleming's garden during the diocesan Garden Fun Day.

The Diocese of Ferns found a creative way to stage a gathering, using Father's Day as inspiration for their family event in Innovate Wexford Park. The day involved live music, a fitness challenge, story telling, and a flower arranging class. Participants were able to meet local sport stars Lee Chin and Mark Fanning, and children could talk to Minnie and Mickey Mouse.

The Diocese of Killaloe held a Family Fun Day at the showgrounds in Ennis, drawings huge crowds for a day full of fun and games. The event featured live music, a bouncy castle, a petting zoo and prizes for the best picnic.

Dioceses also organised lectures and discussions in preparation for WMOF2018, always focusing on the themes of family, marriage and love outlined in the Pope's inspiring apostolic exhortation, *Amoris Laetitia*.

Both the Diocese of Kerry and the Diocese of Kildare & Leighlin hosted special Lenten discussions to encourage parishioners to brainstorm different ideas for incorporating family into their Lenten traditions. Kildare & Leighlin organised discussions on 'The Christian Vision of the Family' and 'Family and Faith' and events related to the sacredness of marriage vows. Married couples in the diocese were also encouraged to renew their vows in a special Mass during the Lenten season.

The Diocese of Derry held more formal discussions during their conference entitled 'A Celebration of Family', which encouraged attendees to get involved in family ministry within their parish or diocese. The Diocese of Limerick also hosted a conference called 'Let's Talk Family: Let's Be Family' that included discussions of *Amoris Laetitia* and talks from experienced community leaders and spiritual directors on how to engage fellow Christians in activities centred on the family in the lead-up to WMOF2018.

Part of the WMOF2018 celebrations in the Diocese of Armagh was a Family Sport Celebration. Here, Archbishop Eamon Martin and Fr Thomas McHugh are seen with children from the diocese playing with a gaelic football. *Photo: www.LiamMcArdle.com*

LEFT: An aerial view of the picnic blankets at the Big Parish Picnic at St Etchen's School, Kinnegad. The picnic attracted many families from all over Meath diocese for a day of family fun. *Photo: Meath Diocese website*

TOP RIGHT: The Diocese of Elphin's Family Picnic was a welcome chance to get outside and play. The event was also a chance for asylum seekers at the local direct provision centre in Sligo to get to know others in the community. *Photo: Elphin Diocese Facebook*

BOTTOM RIGHT: Flags representing each parish in the Kildare and Leighlin diocese flapping in the wind during the diocese's Family Fun Day. *Photo: KandLe Facebook*

Priests from the Diocese of Ferns pose with some of the Family Fun Day's visitors. *Photo: Ferns Diocese*

The launch of the Killaloe Family Fun Day Picnic shows off the tea, cake and entertainment that were featured at the event in Ennis Showgrounds.

The pet farm was a hit at the Archdiocese of Cashel & Emly's Family Fun Day.

NATIONAL OPENING

Tens of thousands of pilgrims from all over Ireland gathered in cathedrals across the country for simultaneous opening ceremonies for the World Meeting of Families across all 26 dioceses on the evening of Tuesday, 21st August, with the lead ceremony taking place in Dublin.

The Opening Liturgy was a full celebration of Evening Prayer, entitled 'Le chéile le Críost' (together with Christ), which aimed to gather the Church as the family of families.

The ceremonies were ecumenical in nature and many Christian Churches joined with their Catholic neighbours in ringing out church bells as the Evening Prayer began all over the island.

Many of the international delegates and speakers also had the opportunity to join local communities across Ireland to celebrate the opening ceremony.

In Dublin, Archbishop Diarmuid Martin presided at Evening Prayer in the RDS – the main site of WMOF which attracted an estimated 37,000 pilgrims for the Pastoral Congress, exhibition and youth events.

Archbishop Martin said that "there are those who would look at the World Meeting as some sort of ideological gathering to celebrate a type of family which probably does not exist.

"Whatever of the past, here in Dublin the World Meeting is something much more profound: it is to reflect the opening words of our reading: 'You are God's chosen race; he loves you'".

Dr Martin said the message "is simple yet profound".

He described the family as the domestic Church before insisting that "the family must be the place where all these dimensions of the Christian life are deepened and lived.

"The family is not a closed place but must always be missionary and have that same drive towards the periphery, towards those who are marginalised, which Pope Francis presents as a fundamental dimension of the Church."

Archbishop Martin said that all present were welcome at the gathering, adding "I greet all the families present in the variety of their expression".

OPPOSITE: Jayden Keaveney, an altar server from Dublin holding a candle during the Opening Ceremony. Parishes throughout the Archdiocese of Dublin joined for a Solemn Evening Prayer to mark the opening of the World Meeting of Families 2018 at the RDS. Sacred Music was led by the Dublin Diocesan Music Group. *Photo: John McElroy/WMOF2018*

TOP LEFT: (L-R) Cardinal Kevin Farrell, Prefect of the Dicastery of Laity, Family and Life speaking with Archbishop of Dublin Diarmuid Martin before the opening ceremony in the RDS, Dublin. *Photo: John McElroy/WMOF2018*

TOP RIGHT: Cardinal Kevin Farrell blessing the incense during the beginning of the opening ceremony. *Photo: John McElroy/WMOF2018*

BOTTOM LEFT: A member of the congregation listening to Pope Francis speaking via video. *Photo: John McElroy/WMOF2018*

OPPOSITE: People listening to Pope Francis' speech at the opening of the World Meeting of Families 2018 at the RDS. *Photo: John McElroy/WMOF2018*

THE GOSPEL OF THE FAMILY

Joy for the World

It is also an occasion for families from all over the world

THIS PAGE: The procession of gifts at the opening ceremony for the Diocese of Ardagh & Clonmacnois celebrated by Bishop Francis Duffy in St Mel's Cathedral in Longford.

OPPOSITE TOP: Parish representatives process into the Cathedral of the Annunciation & St Nathy in Ballaghaderreen at the celebration in Achonry diocese.

OPPOSITE BOTTOM LEFT: Altar servers at the Evening Prayer ceremony in the Diocese of Cloyne, celebrated in St Colman's Cathedral, Cobh by Bishop William Crean.

OPPOSITE BOTTOM RIGHT: Each parish in Cork & Ross diocese were represented by a family who received a WMOF candle to be lit in the Parish Church for the week, at the ceremony in the Cathedral of Ss Mary and Anne, Cork presided by Bishop John Buckley.

The WMOF Opening Ceremony for the Diocese of Derry was celebrated by Bishop Donal McKeown in St Eugene's Cathedral in Derry. The bishop said the week's events in Dublin "are an invitation for us all to reflect. It is not a time for quick, smart answers but for thoughtful listening. It is a moment of divine grace where we can together seek the truth that alone can set us free." *Photos: Stephen Latimer*

TOP: Young volunteers from the Diocese of Kildare & Leighlin at the Evening Prayer led by Bishop Denis Nulty, with Cardinal Peter Turkson as Homilist, in Carlow Cathedral.

BOTTOM: Bishop Ray Browne with Fr Sean Hanafin and Deacon Connor Bradley in the St Mary's Cathedral, Killarney in the Diocese of Kerry.

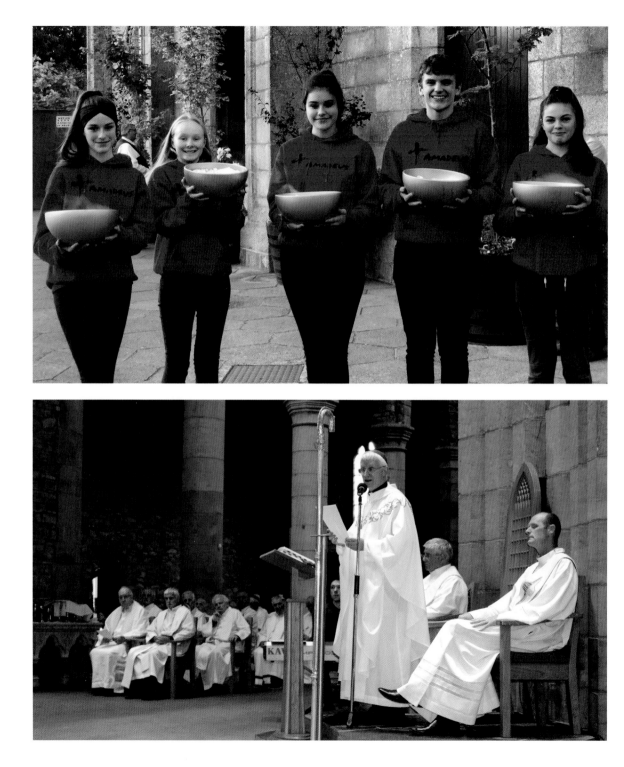

TOP RIGHT: Cistercian sisters from Glencairn Abbey at the Evening Prayer in The Cathedral of The Most Holy Trinity, Waterford.

BOTTOM AND TOP LEFT: Bishop Brendan Leahy chatting to parishioners at a Street Party and Celebration Liturgy in St John's Square, Limerick which was followed by a celebration liturgy at St John's Cathedral.

Scenes from the WMOF Opening Festival in Armagh archdiocese which was followed by music and Evening Prayer led by Archbishop Eamon Martin (pictured right). *Photos: www.LiamMcArdle.com*

TOP LEFT: Young people lead the procession at the Opening Ceremony for the Diocese of Clogher at St Macartan's Cathedral in Monaghan.

TOP RIGHT: Bishop Leo O'Reilly of Kilmore plants a commemorative tree in the grounds of St Ninnidh's Church, Derrylin, Co. Fermanagh, following a diocesan celebration of Solemn Evening Prayer to mark the beginning of WMOF2018. *Photo: Martin McBrien*

LEFT: The Opening Ceremony in the Archdiocese of Cashel & Emly was a Liturgy of Evening Prayer to celebrate the origins of our faith in the Cathedral of the Assumption, Thurles.

TOP RIGHT & LEFT: Parish representatives from the Diocese of Killala at the Opening Service of Prayer in St Muredach's Cathedral, Ballina with a petition box in the shape of a large hand-woven globe, representing our connection to each other across the world.

LEFT: Fr Billy Swan leads the procession of gifts into St Aidan's Cathedral in Wexford for the Opening Ceremony in the Diocese of Ferns.

OPPOSITE LEFT: Participants being welcomed to the Prayer Vigil for the WMOF Opening Ceremony in St Brendan's Cathedral, Loughrea. *Photo: Larry Morgan*

OPPOSITE TOP RIGHT: Bishop Philip Boyce lighting candles at the celebration in Newry Cathedral for the Diocese of Dromore.

OPPOSITE BOTTOM RIGHT: The altar display in Our Lady of the Rosary Church, Nenagh for the Opening Ceremony in the Diocese of Killaloe.

TOP RIGHT: The procession waiting outside St Eunan's Cathedral, Letterkenny for the celebration in the Diocese of Raphoe. *Photo: Noel Ferry*

BOTTOM RIGHT: Bishop Robert Brennan from the Diocese of Rockville Centre, New York was accompanied by 20 lay delegates at Mass for the Opening of the World Meeting of Families, celebrated by Bishop Michael Smith of Meath in the Cathedral of Christ the King, Mullingar.

OPPOSITE: Two boys dressed as Pope Francis share a quiet word at the ceremony in Letterkenny. *Photo: Noel Ferry*

PASTORAL CONGRESS

....

I n his Letter for World Meeting of Families 2018, Pope Francis asked that the event and its preparation would give families the opportunity to deepen their reflection and understanding of the contents of *The Joy of Love* (*Amoris Laetitia*). The programme of the three-day Pastoral Congress in the Royal Dublin Society (RDS) from August 22-24, took up this call.

The congress offered a daily programme of workshops and discussions, two buzzing exhibition halls and many fun and prayerful activities for individuals and families, including a tailored programme for children (4-12 years) and young people (13-17 years). The highlight of each day was the celebration of the Eucharist in the RDS main arena.

A number of the talks, which included both international and Irish speakers, were packed out to capacity including Fr James Martin SJ who gave a workshop on 'Showing Welcome and Respect in our Parishes for 'LGBT' People and their Families' and Bishop Robert Barron who spoke on the theme 'Pope Francis on the Gospel of the Family: What is Jesus Calling our Families to be?'.

OPPOSITE: (L to R) Cardinal Christoph Schonborn, Archbishop of Vienna, Moderator of the panel, Michael Jackson, Church of Ireland, Archbishop of Dublin, Arch Priest Mikhail Nasonov, Rector of the Russian Orthodox, Patriarchal Monastery of the Church of the Holy Apostles Peter and Paul, Dublin and Rabbi Zalman S. Lent, Chief Rabbi, Dublin Hebrew Congregation, Chabad- Lubauitch speaking at the workshop entitled 'In the light of the Word, celebrating family in the Judeo Christian Tradition'. *Photo: John McElroy/WMOF2018*

OPPOSITE LEFT: Dr Eamon Martin, Archbishop of Armagh, Primate of All Ireland giving a speech titled 'Welfare of the Family is decisive for the future of the World'. *Photo: John McElroy/WMOF2018*

OPPOSITE TOP RIGHT: Participants from Canada at the Pastoral Congress. *Photo: John McElroy/WMOF2018*

OPPOSITE BOTTOM RIGHT: Louis Viallon, aged 3, France taking some time out at the Pastoral Congress. *Photo: John McElroy/WMOF2018*

ABOVE: Bishops and cardinals at the afternoon Mass at the main arena at the Pastoral Congress. *Photo: John McElroy/WMOF2018*

TOP LEFT: Marie Collins, former member of the Pontifical Commission for Protection of Minors on the panel discussion titled 'Safeguarding Children and Vulnerable Adults'. *Photo: John McElroy/WMOF2018*

TOP RIGHT: Fr Leo Patalinghug, priest, chef and author doing a cooking demonstration and talk titled 'Grace before Meals. Recipes to strengthen family life'. *Photo: John McElroy/WMOF2018*

BOTTOM RIGHT: Bishop Robert E. Barron, Auxiliary Bishop of the Archdioceses of LA giving a talk titled 'Pope Francis on the gospel of the family. What is Jesus calling our families to be'. *Photo: John McElroy/ WMOF2018*

OPPOSITE TOP: A group from Jersey. *Photo: John McElroy/WMOF2018*

OPPOSITE BOTTOM RIGHT: A group of young people enjoying a break. *Photo: John McElroy/WMOF2018*

OPPOSITE BOTTOM LEFT: Priests from Toledo in Spain. *Photo: John McElroy/WMOF2018*

TOP LEFT: Volunteers at Mass in the main arena. *Photo: John McElroy/WMOF2018*

TOP RIGHT: Cois Na Labhna from Co. Clare providing some music in the grounds of the RDS. *Photo: John McElroy/WMOF2018*

BOTTOM LEFT: Members of the Franciscan Friars, Sisters of Renewal and members of the Holy Family Mission from Waterford. *Photo: John McElroy/WMOF2018*

OPPOSITE TOP: Group of volunteers at the RDS. *Photo: John McElroy/WMOF2018*

OPPOSITE BOTTOM LEFT: Students from Thornhill College Derry. *Photo: John McElroy/WMOF2018*

OPPOSITE BOTTOM LEFT: Sr Anne from Germany with Éirinn the sheep, the mascot of WMOF. *Photo: John McElroy/WMOF2018*

PAPAL ARRIVAL

Some 38 years after he spent three months in Dublin as a Jesuit priest, Jorge Bergoglio returned to Dublin as Pope. Francis was welcomed by high-ranking State and Church officials at Dublin Airport on Saturday morning, August 25th, including Tánaiste Simon Coveney, Primate of All-Ireland Archbishop Eamon Martin, Archbishop Diarmuid Martin of Dublin and Irish Ambassador to the Holy See Emma Madigan. He also met with the Boland family, whose daughter Jane (11), won a competition organised by World Missions Ireland to design a vestment for the Pope.

After brief greetings, he left the airport in the small blue Skoda that was to become his trademark on the trip and travelled to Áras an Uachtaráin where he was greeted by President Michael D. Higgins and his wife Sabina. In their meeting President Higgins and Pope Francis agreed on the importance of protecting vulnerable communities and individuals, at home and abroad and emphasised the importance of measures to prevent and redress all forms of abuse of privilege or power.

The Pontiff was then transferred to Dublin Castle where he met with members of the Government, Civil Society and Diplomatic Corps. In a speech welcoming Pope Francis to Ireland, Taoiseach Leo Varadkar said the Pontiff's visit "marks the opening of a new chapter in the relationship between Ireland and the Catholic Church".

In his speech Pope Francis addressed the issue of clerical abuse, saying it was a "betrayal of trust" by Church authorities, and remains a source of "pain and shame" for the Catholic community, and "I myself share those sentiments".

On his way to St Mary's Pro-Cathedral, the Pope stopped outside Our Lady of Lourdes Church on Sean McDermott Street, which holds Matt Talbot's tomb. Here Francis had a brief meet and greet with well-wishers, before transferring into a white popemobile.

From across Ireland's 26 dioceses, 350 couples filled Dublin's cathedral for the first pastoral portion of Pope Francis' journey to Ireland for the WMOF. His address was described as both humorous and informal, with the Pope telling couples never to go to sleep without resolving conflicts.

Tens of thousands of people lined the streets of Dublin to cheer and catch a glimpse of Pope Francis as he made his way across the city in his popemobile from the pro-cathedral to the Capuchin Day Centre in Smithfield, where he paid tribute to the dignity of the homeless. The Pontiff spoke with the co-director of the centre, Br Kevin Crowley, and thanked him for his charitable work, saying: "The Church has real need of this witness." He met with both service users and volunteers, and offered a blessing to those in attendance.

The Pontiff then met with eight Irish survivors of clerical, religious and institutional abuse for ninety minutes in the Apostolic Nunciature on the Navan Road, where he condemned those who covered up clerical abuse as 'caca' (filth).

That evening Pope Francis completed his first day in Ireland by attending the Festival of Families in Croke Park.

OPPOSITE: Tánaiste and Minister for Foreign Affairs and Trade; Simon Coveney TD, his wife Ruth and his daughters Jessica, Beth and Annalise greet Pope Francis at his arrival at Dublin Airport. *Photo: Maxwells/WMOF2018*

TOP LEFT: Jane Boland (11) from Nenagh, Co. Tipperary, who won a competition to design a vestment for Pope Francis greets the Pontiff on his arrival at Dublin Airport. *Photo: Maxwells/WMOF2018*

TOP RIGHT: Archbishop Diarmuid Martin greets Pope Francis. *Photo: Maxwells/ WMOF2018*

BOTTOM LEFT: Pope Francis and Taoiseach Leo Varadkar greet a child at Dublin Castle. *Photo: Maxwells/WMOF2018*

OPPOSITE: Pope Francis at a tree planting ceremony with President Higgins and his wife Sabina at Áras an Uachtaráin. *Photo: Maxwells/WMOF2018*

Pope Francis addresses 350 couples at St Mary's Pro-Cathedral. *Photo: Maxwells/WMOF2018*

Pope Francis as he departs St Mary's Pro-Cathedral. *Photo: Maxwells/WMOF2018*

OPPOSITE: Pope Francis pictured as the popemobile passes through the crowded streets of Dublin. *Photo: Maxwells/WMOF2018*

TOP: Pope Francis shakes hands with Br Kevin Crowley as he arrives at the Capuchin Day Centre on Bowe Street in Dublin. *Photo: Maxwells/WMOF2018*

BOTTOM: Pope Francis greets Aidan Walsh during his visit to the Capuchin Day Centre. *Photo: Maxwells/WMOF2018*

FESTIVAL OF FAMILIES

Over 80,000 pilgrims from across the generations joined Pope Francis to share and rejoice in their faith, at an array of artistic displays, musical numbers and family testimonies in Croke Park.

The Pontiff arrived at the Festival of Families on Saturday evening, August 25th, to thunderous applause and cheers as his popemobile made its way through the crowd.

Sitting on the stage flanked by Archbishop Diarmuid Martin and Cardinal Kevin Farrell, Francis was treated to a range of Irish and international talent, including the Riverdance troupe, as well as Daniel O'Donnell singing *Let Your Love Flow*, and a rendition of *Ave Maria* by Andrea Bocelli and Celine Byrne.

Between performances, social justice groups and families spoke directly to the Pontiff, explaining the difficulties they have endured, such as Azeez Al-Kanah who recollected his family fleeing their home in Iraq after the Islamic State invaded their village.

Missy Collins of the Pavee Point Traveller group told Francis of the struggles the Traveller community face in Ireland for recognition, and asked for further work to be done so that her community is respected. This serious testimony was followed by a light-hearted moment when 12-year-old Alison Nevin managed to snap a 'selfie' with the Pontiff after he gave her a blessing and some commemorative rosary beads.

When the performances ended, Francis opened his address to the crowds with the words, "Dia daoibh", and then spoke about the importance of the family, with an emphasis on parents baptising their children.

He also focused on the importance of the role of grandparents and warned of the dangers of social media.

The Pope ended his address telling the crowd "see you tomorrow", and encouraged them to have a rest before the papal Mass in the Phoenix Park.

OPPOSITE: Pope Francis makes his way through the crowds at Croke Park. *Photo: Maxwells/WMOF2018*

OPPOSITE: A group of 120 children, including members of the Palestrina Choir, perform the song *True Friend. Photo: Maxwells/WMOF2018*

ABOVE: Pope Francis addressing the Festival of Families. *Photo: Maxwells/WMOF2018*

TOP RIGHT: A child waves a papal flag in Croke Park. *Photo: Maxwells/WMOF2018*

BOTTOM RIGHT: Children pictured as Pope Francis makes his way through the crowd at the Festival of Families. *Photo: Maxwells/WMOF2018*

TOP LEFT: Nuns take a selfie as Pope Francis arrives at Croke Park. *Photo: Maxwells/ WMOF2018*

TOP RIGHT: Cardinal Kevin Farrell and Pope Francis enjoying the performances. *Photo: Maxwells/WMOF2018*

BOTTOM RIGHT: Pope Francis meets Nisha, Ted and their family who travelled from India to share their testimony on the affects of technology on the family. *Photo: Maxwells/ WMOF2018*

OPPOSITE TOP: Pope Francis addresses the large crowd. *Photo: Maxwells/WMOF2018*

OPPOSITE BOTTOM LEFT: Singer Daniel O'Donnell performs at Croke Park. *Photo: Maxwells/WMOF2018*

OPPOSITE BOTTOM RIGHT: Riverdance performers dancing for Pope Francis. *Photo: Maxwells/WMOF2018*

LEFT: Sr Martina Purdy, an Adoration Sister from Belfast, waving a papal flag. *Photo: Greg Daly/The Irish Catholic*

TOP RIGHT: Some of the crowd dancing while they await the arrival of Pope Francis. *Photo: John Mc Elroy/WMOF2018*

OPPOSITE: Pope Francis gives the thumbs up to a group of young Irish dancers. *Photo: John Mc Elroy/WMOF2018*

> "It is good to celebrate, for celebration makes us more human and more Christian."

POPE FRANCIS
Croke Park, 25th August, 2018

TOP: WMOF volunteers joining in with the dancing. *Photo: Greg Daly/The Irish Catholic*

BOTTOM: A section of the 80,000 crowd in Croke Park. *Photo: Greg Daly/The Irish Catholic*

OPPOSITE TOP: Young performers relaxing backstage. *Photo: Greg Daly/The Irish Catholic*

OPPOSITE BOTTOM LEFT: Fr Alan Neville from Missionaries of the Sacred Heart at Croke Park. *Photo: Greg Daly/The Irish Catholic*

OPPOSITE BOTTOM RIGHT: A group of young performers huddle on stage. *Photo: Greg Daly/The Irish Catholic*

KNOCK SHRINE

Pope Francis arrived at Ireland West Airport on Sunday, August 26th on an Aer Lingus flight aptly named EI1979, a reference to St John Paul II's visit in 1979. He spent an hour and a half at Ireland's national Marian shrine in Knock, where he led pilgrims in the Angelus Prayer after a period of silent reflection at the Apparition chapel.

Pope Francis described clerical abuse as an "open wound" and begged God for forgiveness for "these sins and for the scandal and betrayal felt by so many others in God's family".

"I ask our Blessed Mother to intercede for the healing of the survivors and to confirm every member of our Christian family in the resolve never again to permit these situations to occur."

Going off script, Francis referred to the separation of children from their mothers, in an apparent reference to Ireland's Mother and Baby Homes which was brought up at a meeting with clerical abuse survivors the day before.

Preparation for the papal visit to Knock began at 8.25am when the bells of Knock Shrine where rung out. The event focused on the story of Knock through the testimony of the witnesses to the 1879 apparition and Pope Francis' invitation to witness to the joy of faith and family in the contemporary world. Music for the occasion was provided by Knock Parish Choir with guest musicians and soloists.

Francis was joined by Archbishop Michael Neary of Tuam in his popemobile as he moved through the crowds waving blue Marian flags. He met the Shrine Rector, Fr Richard Gibbons and presented him with a golden rosary for the shrine, saying he knows how "important the tradition of the family rosary has been in this country". In return the Pontiff was gifted a replica of a section of the mosaic in the basilica depicting the apparition.

Although there wasn't a visit to the north of Ireland on the Pope's itinerary, he addressed this by sending "a warm greeting to the beloved people of Northern Ireland".

In a post-Angelus address he also offered a special greeting to men and women in Ireland's prison system, especially thanking those who wrote to him when they heard of his visit to Ireland.

OPPOSITE: Pope Francis greets pilgrims at Knock Shrine. *Photo: Maxwells/WMOF2018*

TOP LEFT: On arriving at Knock Airport, Pope Francis is presented with flowers by Saoirse McCarthy (11) from St Patrick's National School, Cloonlyon, Co. Mayo. *Photo: Maxwells/WMOF2018*

TOP RIGHT & BOTTOM RIGHT: Pilgrims awaiting the arrival of Pope Francis in the rain at Knock Shrine. *Photo: Maxwells/WMOF2018*

OPPOSITE: Students from St Patrick's National School, Cloonlyon, Co. Mayo awaiting the arrival of Pope Francis. *Photo: Maxwells/WMOF2018*

OPPOSITE: Crowds at Knock Shrine wave as Pope Francis passes in his popemobile. *Photo: Maxwells/WMOF2018*

TOP LEFT: Pope Francis in silent prayer in the Apparition Chapel. *Photo: Maxwells/WMOF2018*

TOP RIGHT: Crowds greeting the arrival of Pope Francis at Knock Shrine. *Photo: Maxwells/WMOF2018*

BOTTOM RIGHT: Pope Francis and Shrine Rector, Fr Richard Gibbons greet pilgrims in the Apparition Chapel. *Photo: Maxwells/WMOF2018*

> "I am happy to be here with you. I am happy to be with you in the house of Our Lady. And I thank God for this opportunity, in the context of the World Meeting of Families, to visit this Shrine, so dear to the Irish people."

POPE FRANCIS
Knock Shrine, 26th August 2018

RIGHT: Pope Francis blesses children dressed as witnesses to the apparition in 1879. *Photo: Maxwells/WMOF2018*

OPPOSITE: Scenes from the crowd waiting for Pope Francis to speak. *Photo: Maxwells/WMOF2018*

Pope Francis smiles during a light moment. *Photo: Maxwells/WMOF2018*

The crowd outside Knock Basilica cheer as Pope Francis passes in his popemobile. *Photo: Maxwells/WMOF2018*

CLOSING MASS

··

Even wind and rain couldn't dampen the spirits of up to 300,000 pilgrims who made their way to Dublin's Phoenix Park on Sunday, August 26th, where a carnival atmosphere surrounded the closing Mass of the ninth World Meeting of Families.

A host of performers ranging from Audrey Assad and Eimear Quinn, to Daniel O'Donnell and the Northern Irish Rend Collective entertained pilgrims before and after the Mass in the Park's fifteen acres, with children breaking out into dance at the fringes of the gathering.

The opening hymn to the Mass was Ephrem Feeley's *A Joy for all the Earth*, the official hymn of WMOF2018, sung by a 3,000-strong choir, and then ceremonies took on a sombre tone, as Pope Francis read in Spanish from a handwritten note he had penned that morning, begging forgiveness for abuses committed by members of the Church.

"We ask forgiveness for the cases of abuse in Ireland, the abuse of power, the abuse of conscience and sexual abuse on the part of representatives of the Church," he said, after having reflected on what he had been told the previous evening by eight survivors of clerical or institutional abuse.

Fr Liam Lawton's psalm *The Lord Hears the Cry of the Poor*, written especially for WMOF2018, followed the first reading, which was read in Irish from the book of Joshua by Clontarf's Marie Whelan, who worked on the new Irish translation of the Mass.

The second reading, from St Paul's Letter to the Ephesians, was read in the Pope's native Spanish by the Argentina-born Teresa Menendez, marketing manager of WMOF2018.

Dublin's Deacon Paul McHugh read from the Gospel of John, with the Pope then stepping into his traditional role of confirming his brethren in their faith, encouraging those gathered to hold to their faith even if it seemed hard. "I think of St Columbanus, who with his small band of companions brought the light of the Gospel to the lands of Europe in an age of darkness and cultural dissolution," he said, explaining that their "extraordinary missionary success" was based on the promptings of the Holy Spirit.

"It was their daily witness of fidelity to Christ and to each other that won hearts yearning for a word of grace and helped give birth to the culture of Europe. That witness remains a perennial source of spiritual and missionary renewal for God's holy and faithful people," the Pontiff said.

The Apostles' Creed was then sung to John O'Keefe's own composition, with Fr Pat Ahern's *A Thiarna Éist Linn* being sung between the Prayers of the Faithful.

Olive Foley, widow of former Munster coach Anthony Foley, and mother-of-five Emma Mhic Mhathuna, accompanied by their children, were among those who brought up gifts in the Offertory Procession, to the strains of Z. Randall Stroope's *Caritas et Amor*, with the bread and wine then placed on the altar beside an 18th-Century penal cross.

OPPOSITE: An aerial view of the Phoenix Park during the WMOF closing Mass. *Photo: Maxwells/WMOF2018*

After the consecration, priests filed out among the people, with yellow umbrellas marking those whose ciboria contained gluten-free bread as Communion was shared with over a quarter of a million people.

Several hymns later, the priests returned to their seats for the closing of the ceremony. Cardinal Kevin Farrell announced that the next World Meeting of Families will be held in Rome, the Pope gave his final blessing, and the Mass ended, while the festivities continued as the crowds trailed out to take the message of WMOF2018 to their families and communities.

After a meeting with Irish bishops at the Dominican Convent, Cabra, Pope Francis then travelled to Dublin Airport where he bid farewell to religious and political leaders, waving to the small gathering as he boarded his flight back to Rome.

RIGHT: Larry Cassidy (11) smiles through the bad weather conditions at the Phoenix Park. *Photo: Maxwells/WMOF2018*

OPPOSITE TOP LEFT: Patrick Maughan Sr and Patrick Maughan Jr (6) awaiting the Pope's arrival. *Photo: Maxwells/WMOF2018*

OPPOSITE TOP RIGHT: Sr Breige McLaughlain, Sr Philomena Folse CFR; Mother Lucile Cutrone CFR; Sr Teresa Dunphy OP; Sr Kelly Francis Oslin CFR; Sr Maria Grace Byars CFR; Sr Cathy Howard OP. *Photo: Maxwells/WMOF2018*

OPPOSITE BOTTOM LEFT: Pilgrims take 'selfies' at the Papal Cross. *Photo: Maxwells/WMOF2018*

OPPOSITE BOTTOM RIGHT: Retired parish priest, Fr Leo Quinlan, from Skerries, Co. Dublin warms up with a hot flask of tea. *Photo: Maxwells/WMOF2018*

Pope Francis arrives at the Phoenix Park.
Photo: Maxwells/WMOF2018

OPPOSITE: Pilgrims await the Pope's arrival for the closing Mass. *Photo: Maxwells/ WMOF2018*

TOP LEFT: Pope Francis arrives at the Phoenix Park. *Photo: Maxwells/WMOF2018*

BOTTOM LEFT: Pilgrims photograph the Pope on their mobile phones as he passes. *Photo: Maxwells/WMOF2018*

TOP RIGHT: Pope Francis waves to pilgrims. *Photo: Maxwells/WMOF2018*

BOTTOM RIGHT: An Taoiseach Leo Varadkar, President Micheal D. Higgins and Mrs Sabina Higgins. *Photo: Maxwells/WMOF2018*

OPPOSITE TOP: Clergy and pilgrims stand for the opening of the Mass. *Photo: Maxwells/WMOF2018*

OPPOSITE BOTTOM LEFT: Members of the Defence Forces at the Phoenix Park Mass. *Photo: Maxwells/WMOF2018*

OPPOSITE BOTTOM RIGHT: Clergy process into the Mass. *Photo: Maxwells/WMOF2018*

OPPOSITE TOP: Church of Ireland Archbishop of Dublin, Dr Michael Jackson at the closing Mass. *Photo: Maxwells/WMOF2018*

OPPOSITE BOTTOM LEFT & RIGHT: Pilgrims enjoying the atmosphere at the Phoenix Park. *Photo: Maxwells/WMOF2018*

ABOVE: Marie Whelan reads the first reading from the book of Joshua in Irish. *Photo: Maxwells/WMOF2018*

Aerial view of the Phoenix Park Mass. Photo: Maxwells/WMOF2018

> "At the end of this World Meeting of Families, we gather as a family around the table of the Lord. We thank God for the many blessings we have received in our families."

POPE FRANCIS
Phoenix Park, 26th August, 2018

OPPOSITE: Pope Francis holds up the Bible after the Gospel reading. *Photo: Maxwells/WMOF2018*

TOP LEFT: The cross used on altar for the closing Mass is a penal cross dating back to 1763 which tells the story of the passion and resurrection of Jesus. *Photo: Maxwells/WMOF2018*

BOTTOM LEFT: Members of the congregation share the sign of peace. *Photo: Maxwells/WMOF2018*

ABOVE: The procession of gifts at the closing Mass. *Photo: Maxwells/WMOF2018*

TOP LEFT: Pope Francis celebrating the Eucharist. *Photo: Maxwells/WMOF2018*

BOTTOM LEFT: A priest distributes Communion. *Photo: Maxwells/WMOF2018*

OPPOSITE: Priests move out to distribute Communion. *Photo: Maxwells/WMOF2018*

OPPOSITE: An aerial view of the closing Mass. *Photo: Maxwells/WMOF2018*

TOP: Pope Francis leaving the Phoenix Park. *Photo: Maxwells/WMOF2018*

BOTTOM: President Micheal D. Higgins and Mrs Sabina Higgins wave goodbye to the crowd. *Photo: Maxwells/WMOF2018*

OPPOSITE TOP LEFT: Pope Francis wishes Archbishop Diarmuid Martin farewell at Dublin Airport. *Photo: Maxwells/WMOF2018*

OPPOSITE TOP RIGHT: Pope Francis shakes hands with Taoiseach Leo Varadkar at Dublin Airport. *Photo: Maxwells/WMOF2018*

OPPOSITE BOTTOM LEFT: Pope Francis says goodbye to Cardinal Seán Brady. *Photo: Maxwells/WMOF2018*

OPPOSITE BOTTOM RIGHT: Pope Francis shakes hands with Sgt. Bernard Young of Ballymun Garda Station at Dublin Airport. *Photo: Maxwells/ WMOF.*

RIGHT: Pope Francis waves as he boards his flight at the end of his two-day visit. *Photo: Maxwells/WMOF2018*

May the road rise up to meet you.

May the wind be always at your back.

May the sun shine warm upon your face;

the rains fall soft upon your fields

and until we meet again,

may God hold you in the palm of His hand.

TRADITIONAL IRISH BLESSING